FROM HERE
TO THERE

an indescribable point in time

ARiA JACKSON

From Here to There
Copyright © 2025 by Aria Jackson.

MILTON & HUGO L.L.C.
4407 Park Ave., Suite 5
Union City, NJ 07087, USA

Website: *www. miltonandhugo.com*
Hotline: *1- 888-778-0033*
Email: *info@miltonandhugo.com*

Ordering Information:
Quantity sales. Special discounts are granted to corporations, associations, and other organizations. For more information on these discounts, please reach out to the publisher using the contact information provided above.

Library of Congress Control Number: IN-PROCESS
ISBN-13:   979-8-89285-733-8   [Paperback Edition]
                  979-8-89285-732-1   [Digital Edition]

Rev. date: 12/03/2025

This book is for all the trapped words buried deep in the notes app, in a coffee stained journal, on a napkin, singing in the mind… Let them free. Embrace the release. Thank you to everyone who amplified my voice and guided me when I was lost. These poems are for you.

Contents

Alliteration

A literal nation of
Lateral notions that
Light the way for useless potions

A lateral ocean.
That stretches through steep
Stations of stolen land
We owe them
We owe them
We owe them our
God given devotion

A better plan that
Places with no complacent purpose
Can repopulate the impatient
Part of our nation
We won't desert them.

We take notes and
Take the tape of our tailored
Vision and talent and
Drop it into the ocean
And top it off with a token

That speaks through speakers
Who speed through the world
Of cheaters and write with emotion

I spilled my daiquiri in the ocean...

Held

I want to be held
To be someone's most precious possession
Deeply valued and overly protected
The person they can't live without

Wrapped in their arms so tight our heartbeats fall in sync
Engrossed in the same rhythm
With one blink, there's trust that I can protect him for the tenth of a
second he can't see
I want unfiltered comfort
Two fish together and the wonders of the sea

To be held together as a root is to tree
That's what I imagine when I dream of you and me

Es- E- Ex

We lock eyes
lock lips
the night is young
hands roam to unseen places.

Carried overhead with ease
A light whisper
"I love you"
Steaming hot skin pancake flat

A vulnerable point
"...beautiful"
Insecurities reassured.

Luscious lips drift down the crease of my stomach
Breaths in rhythm
suctioned air
A full body experience

I'm on top, but he's higher
no failure, no doubt
I have his heart.

It beats sporadically but its endured
It climbs every wall I build
It loves deeper than physical connection
It beats louder to whispers of my voice.

A Wilted Rose

A wilted rose I held on to
Just for fun
Passing by it daily
Watching it transform

The color darkened to something unrecognizable
The petals drained of energy
Ants seeping from corners of the desk
To comfort a lone flower

What's so hard about letting go?
Why didn't I put it out of its misery?
Throw the rose away?
I squashed ant by ant to protect its dignity
To salvage what little life was left

But the weight the rose carried was to heavy to release
I held on to it
I knew it was still fighting
Hate to lose hope for a fighter

Eventually I let it go.
Patience grew short for pests and extra burdens
I held on to it as long as I could
Because if I'd let it go too early,
It wouldn't have been ready

There's beauty in timing
And the wilted flower I held on to
ran out of time

Focus

I can't focus. I can't fix my mind to stay on topic because there's a
flashing red screen replaying the bloodiest images of my people
being murdered that's etched in my brain. I wish I didn't know the
truth. I'm scared. I'm scared to check my notifications on instagram
out of fear that I'll come across another black woman's name
diminished to a hashtag. From the moment I wake up to the time my
eyes surrender at night I am running. Running like my life depends
on it. Running in the marathon called life. All of us beside each
other trying to achieve this never felt state of triumph. A victory and
success that no human can take away from you. Just gotta finish
what feels like an impossible race.

Somedays I sprint, to speed up the process
Somedays I speed walk to pass by the white supremacists plotting
my downfall
Sometimes I jog, when I'm overwhelmed by the chaos
surrounding me
Most days I just sit, stuck, thinking I'm too damn tired.

Too tired of explaining to others why my life matters too
Too tired of having to amplify my own voice in a room full of people
who don't even acknowledge my presence
Too tired of the pressure to compete with my fellow black women for
limited opportunities
Too tired of holding back tears at the ignorance of my uneducated
peers
Tired of easing the fury and rage in my blood at the sound of the
President's voice
Tired of suppressing my passion to not be stereotyped as the Angry
Black Woman
Tired of biting my tongue to be considerate of the white man's
feelings

Tired of being a soldier fighting in this never-ending race war
Tired of being tired.
Tired of running in this damn race.

Most days my self motivation isn't enough. My focus is distorted by
the black women beside me dropping like flies at hands of the law.
I think of when we were all lined up in the beginning of the race, I
remember their faces. Pay tribute to those who we've lost. I look at
the empty lanes of Breonna Taylor and Atatiana Jefferson and think,
I keep running for you.

I won't stop.

Stop Kiss

Everything stopped...
leaving me stuck on an island
in waters I can't swim in

Forced to face my fears
Only to realize my biggest fear is myself.
Breaking the barrier of "self-discipline"
Engage in social interaction

it's been 282 days since I've kissed someone
and way over a year since one has had meaning.

I miss humans.
Had the world not been on pause
I'd be a different person

For better or for worse
I need to stop holding myself back
and just fucking kiss someone

Me Who Was Stuck

Do you ever just stop and stare?
Float into the abyss
Feel the cool breeze on your back?
Walk with no destination in mind
Shrink into your own world
With tunnel vision so vague
The only identifiable thing is that path

That sidewalk of uncertainty
The chatter around you dissipates into white noise
And only you are left
Blank
Confused
Floating
In your metaphysical mind

There's something in the distance.
My mind runs to get close to it
It's me.
Stuck
Staring into space

I'm here?
But I'm not.
She's there

Just like that time catches up
Washes away my parallel universe
I'm awakened by voices
More superfluous than before

Reality struck
Me who was stuck

Barely Lit Bud

Outside my window
and across the street
The smoke of a lit cigarette
travels to me
It's personified aura
Silently screams
The force of the wind
Gray clouds fade retreat
A squirrel hopping
Amongst the branches of a tree
Standing tall with a sturdy
Foundation underneath
Another puff
And the smoke and I, again, desire to meet
Through the window, across the median
Separated by concrete
It's thin, loose entity
Wants to be set free
So come to me!
Use more heat
Puff puff
Inhale, repeat
Quit being so damn discreet
And travel to where our ends can meet
With the quickness of the breeze
you settle in defeat
No strength to fight the wind
And no energy to compete
Outside the window
and across the street
The barely lit bud
Got smushed by two feet

Starry Night's Flight

T'was indeed a starry starry night
Sky's pattern guided by the swift wind
Blue moonlight shone iridescent bright
Deep breath in awe, our arms extend

My hand in his, staring at the view
Towns and oceans a short distance away
I open my eyes to a dream come true
My toes aligned to the stars' array

Together we stand, towering the night
Hand in hand, anticipating our flight
The illusion of the night, trapped on a sheet
Pulled back into reality, grounded by our feet

We say our goodbyes to the painting
And thank great Van Gogh for the acquaintance

If the Heroine was Heard

From the perspective of Shakespeare's heroines Portia, Juliet and Hermia.

Marry is the very theme
How stands your disposition to be married?
An Honour
A Dream
It is an honour that I dream not of.

Love
Volume of beauty's pen
Examine
How one another lends content

Easy
Instructions
Follow mine own teaching,
O me, the word "choose"
Will
Living daughter
Will
Dead father
I can not choose one nor refuse none?

Enemy
Art thyself
O, be some other name!
What's in a name?
Perfection?
A Title?
Take all myself.

Your grace,

Pardon me
I know not by what power I am made bold.
Plead my thoughts,
The worst case
If I refuse
Grow
Live
Die.
My soul consents…

Shrooms

truly a trip
comfort
stillness
lost time
color.

pink hue
glistening
water
shakes,
wave.

berhana
foushee
let her sing
hand hug
cold.

I Hate Bras

Sorry if this offends you
But I hate wearing a bra

I receive death stares in awe
Just because I'm not wearing a bra

I don't care if it makes your skin crawl
I don't need to wear a bra

So turn the cheek and close your jaw
Look, that woman's wearing a bra!

There's nothing in the written law
suggesting a declaration of the bra

It doesn't matter how raw or what you saw,
Beauty doesn't lie in the wires of a bra

So no dude, don't pass me a shawl
to cover up the fact I'm not wearing a bra

I promise you it isn't the last straw
Accept my heart not shielded by a bra

But next time you associate comfort with a flaw
Go spend $25 and stuff your chest in a bra

Too Fast a Clock

A tick, a shift, time passes fast
No control of the present
Another minute wasted.

Another minute, wasted.
Sixty entire seconds emptied into the void
How pointless the seconds of my silence tasted

A tick, a shift, time passed quickly
The loser to a battle
with the hands of a quickie

Grappling with questions, keep moving I assume
the ticking grows faster
In a circle, dizzy hands zoom

Tick, another second, tick, goes around
I wish the goddamn hands would fall down
And stop and slow down and pause, I frown

Time speeds up and I'm behind a lap
My legs slower than the hands of the beast
A click, a shift, time surely passed fast
another minute wasted, exhausted in disbelief.

You stole a pizza my heart

About time I left home. I hopped on my
bike headed east on West
Carroll street over the
deepest potholes on the block.
Evening rose, I pedaled
faster, blasting the one and only
Grandmaster Flash in the confines of my walkman.
"Hi Mr. Ellis!" I shouted. His arm vigorously waved from his porch.
"I saw your boy earlier, he was looking for you" Mr. Ellis said.
"Ja-- Jack's Diner" we said simultaneously. "You better hurry up,
Kid's been waiting there for a minute."
"Look here, I'm going!" I yelled as I put
my headphones on and pumped the pedals with pressure.
No one understood the anger I felt. It's almost 8
O'clock. Our meeting time was 6. He
Probably left already. I just need him to answer one
question for me. To make matters worse, three
rain drops just dripped down the side of my face. Through the blur
of my tears,
street lines fade then disappear. Struggling to see in the
thick of the night, I approached the dimly lit diner sign.
Under an umbrella, holding soaked flowers and a box of soggy pizza
Victor appeared from the side of the building.
"What is all this?" I said in tears, opening a hand written card that
reads
'XO-XO, You stole a pizza my heart... Love V'. We stopped for a
moment.
"You said love, V?" I asked, staring into his eyes. "Yes, I love you
more than I love sweets"
Zoned out from the world around us, we kissed in the rain and our
hearts skipped beats.

Me Vs. Them

A girl
Barred but oh so
Clever sits on a step in the corner.
Despondent by
Exhausting conversations on the surface. She
Forgot where she came from. A
Girl from right outside Chocolate City, a nice
Hood, she'd call it. PG County bred. PG County fed.
It was home. Comforting faces, the
Jackson family, a 20 minute drive away.
Kids looked like me, acted
Like
Me. I was
Never alone
Out of place or
Pushed under the rug. Here I'm not under the rug, maybe a nicely crocheted
Quilt, or just a blanket of discomfort.
Remembering the stomach pained laughter of fun or the
Songs that we shouted at the
Top of our lungs, only we- resonated with.
Under their breath they say the word they can't say. I say it with pride, with my
Volume accelerated because- I can.
WE can. They take
Xanax before class. Which is
Y I am sitting on the step in the corner.
Zealous with words that differentiate me from them.

BLACK BEING

14 children died in a school shooting in Texas yesterday.
The same state that is trying to abolish abortions and control
women's bodies.
The same state that banned a children's book for "teaching critical
race theory."
Hey fuck the little black kids.
Representation is obsolete.
Representation is off the screen.
Representation is make believe.
Make believe your future.
I mean culture.
No representation for you.

Texas is the same state where you can get a gun before you turn 21.
Mispelling g-i-n for gun.
Texas says fuck Reg-u-la-tion.

My insta feed fed me a video of a white officer shooting a black man,
an innocent black man,
an unarmed innocent black man.
Within three seconds of arriving on site.
Who's black skin, black soul, black essence, black being,
read threat? Read villain? Read danger? Read
FUCK YOU LAW.
That polices the streets of our neighborhoods and shoots humans
like darts. Bodies
on carts, on a stand. Don't stand. Take my hand.
We flee to the motherland... Said Frank into the Ocean

(hums the melody of 'Wade in the Water')

Down by the river by the hankee pankee
where a kid got shot by blue in a hankee
in the east, west coast, blink, precinct
my favorite friend gone.

(LIGHTS OUT)

Casualty

What happens when an opportunity arises?
Something that crossed your mind too many times to ignore
Something you dreamed of on a naughty day
Something deep down you wished for...

It floats, he floats
And one day lands
Exactly where I hoped he'd be
His chest in my hands

As we live out my sexiest fantasy
Except I- really care what he thinks of me
Fear I- won't live up to satisfactory
See- that's the saddest fact for me
Cause- last night I saw his mastery
In- timidation sat in my soul right after he...

He is patient
Respectful
Attentive
Sexy
A hopeless romantic
10 things I hate about you
Turned me hopeless to
Any thoughts of romance with you

This is to be casual...
Casual
I've got to stop thinking so rational
That we can build this ever so gradual-ly
I have to remember that this is casual

Suppress
Deep breath
Don't stress

I can feel myself becoming a casualty laying on his chest.

Piece of My Father

Inspired by the Paramount movie "Gully"

Remembering the last words from /dad/ who
died. Watching as his /blood/ dripped
down the driver seat window

Splattered by the last piece of
/my father/ I stared at /my
reflection/ in the rear view mirror

To the arcade to /blast/ some
heads off in GTA. I ask the boys
which /weapon/ will I use today.

Jesse /beat/ the high score
in /silence/ I've never heard him speak.
He never knew his /father./

The metal gate flung open and dad
ran in, full force, with his /fist raised /
pounding on the closest /skin/ to him

Nicky's dad, would /hit and run/
until he was dragged by policemen
never to be seen again.

I was seven,
Nicky was eight and
Jesse doesn't /remember./

Although he's not here
I still hear his voice in my head
"If you want something, you better /take it"/

Which /weapon/ should we use today?
Jesse selected a /club/
So we took one, found a guy with a truck

/Smashed/ the window
Beat the owner to a /pulp/
/Jumped/ in the car and began our ride

/Adrenaline/ rushed through our veins,
Filled the truck full with /ferocious laughter/
as the wind /punched/ the dry /blood/ on our faces.

Racing down the back road to no set
destination, I look at /my reflection/ in the driver seat mirror
and see a piece of /my father./

Night Drive

It's dangerous out there
Driving with something heavy on your mind
The road once filled with traffic and cars
Empty
Every light I pull up to turns green
And there's nothing to do but go
Drive on that empty road
The speed limit
Not fast
Not slow
I can't see the cars
Or the gas station prices
Or if McDonalds had a long line
All I saw was the gray
Solid pavement
Telling me to stay within the yellow dotted lines
Don't stray too far left or right
My only task was going straight
Making it home safely
The bumps and lifts in the road met my sunken level
The potholes were filled with my worries
I cruised smoothly down the empty road
With every care in the world
Too much care for the world
Not enough for me

Will I make it home?
Is it just me out here?
Can anyone see me?
Is this light supposed to be red?

I fit perfectly into my parking spot
Lifted my numb fingers glued to the steering wheel
Broke my daze to grab the keys from the ignition
I made it home
But am I safe?

Love Trauma

Dear Trauma,

his dad left, mine did too.
stereotyped, followed in the store.
fear, of that laser red target on our back.
nightmares, dying by a police's gun.
broken teeth of my comb, his locked up coils.
thickness, Blackness, so much strength.
bred body, endures the stares of strangers.
hums the power of a plantation's amazing graces
cook for him, cook for 3, responsibility mom left me.
his meals of choice reek of grief.
chitterlings and peas,
soothed with chamomile tea,
reminder, that we are free.
prayer at night for protection
pray for happiness
salute the weight our bodies carry
the exact reason why we'll marry

//

We've been called names that aren't our own and been expected to respond.

We've lived in poverty but didn't know that's what it was called until we learned the cost of free

We've shaded our bandaids with markers so people can't see we've been bruised.

We colored our faces in coloring books with tan crayons because I already colored the dirt brown and we were Black.

We learned that Black should be upper case when referring to our people because we are not little.

We discovered when we stand beside each other we could never be riddled. It took years to understand that our voices had power. That the ripple of our cries together could make hate cripple.

That we could think thoughts different than what was taught in our history books.

When we learned there is a thing called Black history. When we realized we are Black making history. When we found out his story isn't ours.

When we came together to write our own...

Sincerely,
Your Lover

Excessive Force

They used excessive force
They grabbed and threw
Tossed and gripped
Held and punched
Kicked and dragged

They stomped and spat
Swung and flung
a man up against a wall
Stretched his back over the fence
where his fingertips grazed the back of his ankles

His back looks broken
My heart is broken

Then dragged him by his locs across the ground
He was kicked and beaten
Before he was placed under arrest.
Before the handcuffs were forced on his wrists
Before he got to say his name
Before he realized his next breath was their aim

They used excessive force to reinstate power
Hiding behind armor, their dignity cowers
Over the shameless body on the ground
And the reason for arrest? Nowhere to be found.

Coachella Day 1

In a jeep,
windows rolled down
sights through purple-tinted glass.

We roll,   roll down hills   Traffic filled city

Shades on

       a breeze whispers around my neck
           "We're going to Coachella!"

Stockler Rd,   a blinking traffic light,   caused the 25 minute delay

minute delay   words delayed

Don't lay,   too long,   just yet

Smoking citrus circus
           Headed East on I-10

The bass moves my chest, Kaytranada

                   I spy a Tesla

"Don't shoot"
    Isaiah Rashad

Leaving Coachella

11:11
Meets the intersection of
Contact & Flashbacks
"Shout out to the ones that accept me for me...
you might catch a contact if you f* around with me"
&
"But I do believe in God and it's odd but I know that even
when I'm strayin' far away from my path there's a reason"

Song reflects my upbringings
I'm up bringing
stuck bringing
Light
to a life
That's corrupt and uptight
Don't feel like the fight
Won't sleep til it's right,
Said leaving a Coachella site...

My life is blessed
And I'm thankful
God poured his soul in me
And I'm grateful

2:22
Passed the Inglewood Crenshaw exit
Maybe this can be my new home?

"Why did the orphan eat cereal with water?"
"Cause his dad never came back with no milk!"
"Don't tell nobody else that joke man"

Kid maybe 14-16
Standing
Jocin
the security guard outside
Med Men
I said my
Medicine
Met when
Anxiety says when
I need to puff puff pass
Deep through the stash
Fill the need to crash
Big clash
With reality

Back to the men outside
Kid's wearing red pants and busted Js
Black hoodie with hair in a temp fade
A skeletal butterfly stretched across the chest
An X ray
His name could be X
Or Jay B
May be
I don't know the story

Maybe that's his brother
To work he goes
So he says
Stay where you know
I get off at 3
Don't stray in the streets
Just come stay by me
We can just be
Be
Free
Stay by me
—Please
I'll slide you a jay or 3.

Maybe.
JB?

3:33
Bag breaking the circulation of my blood
Doesn't flow
This line
Doesn't flow
My spine
Doesn't grow
Fingers tingling
Heavy handles hurt

Moechella

Coachella Coachella
Moechella Fauxchella

Ima go getta
Ticket to Coachella

Dessert sand in my eye
Sweat dripping down my thigh
Hot as hell, titties cry
Bra made cage inside

There was a moment I held back tears
I felt a range of emotions
Paused in my motion
Lost my breath
The room circled like an ocean
Amidst the commotion
A white kid tried to touch my hair
I couldn't look him in the eye
My throat choked on a cry
No words to explain why
So I
Reached for my friends who weren't there
Leaned on the wood, eyes caught in a stare
My back slid down the retched shack
Feet stretched out in front of me
Heart palpitations and I sat there
Struggling to breathe

A white girl came and took a picture of me
She thought I didn't see
I was just trying to breathe
I stood up on 3

They called my name
I grabbed my food
And walked through the crowded sea
I found my friends
Ate my food and didn't say a peep

Fate

While we wait
      Hearts beating at an unsteady rate
            A group of 7 determines the fate
                        Justice or Hate?

'1960 Change / ChangeMakers' photographed by Troy Pierre II

'Loose Change' shot by Troy Pierre II

'Reflections' photographed by Troy Pierre II

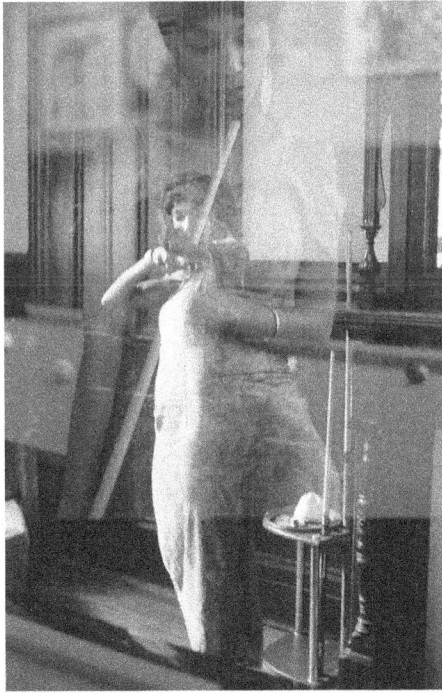

'Shots' photographed by Troy Pierre II

39

'A Wilted Rose' taken by me

'You Stole A Pizza My Heart' photographed by Will Willoughby

'Cries for Gaza' taken by my friend Matt Thompson Jr.

'Monday at Sunset'

'Coachella 2023'

'If the Heroine was Heard' taken by an anonymous photographer

'Flight' photographed by Doug Spearman

Photographed by La'Shance Perry. June 2025

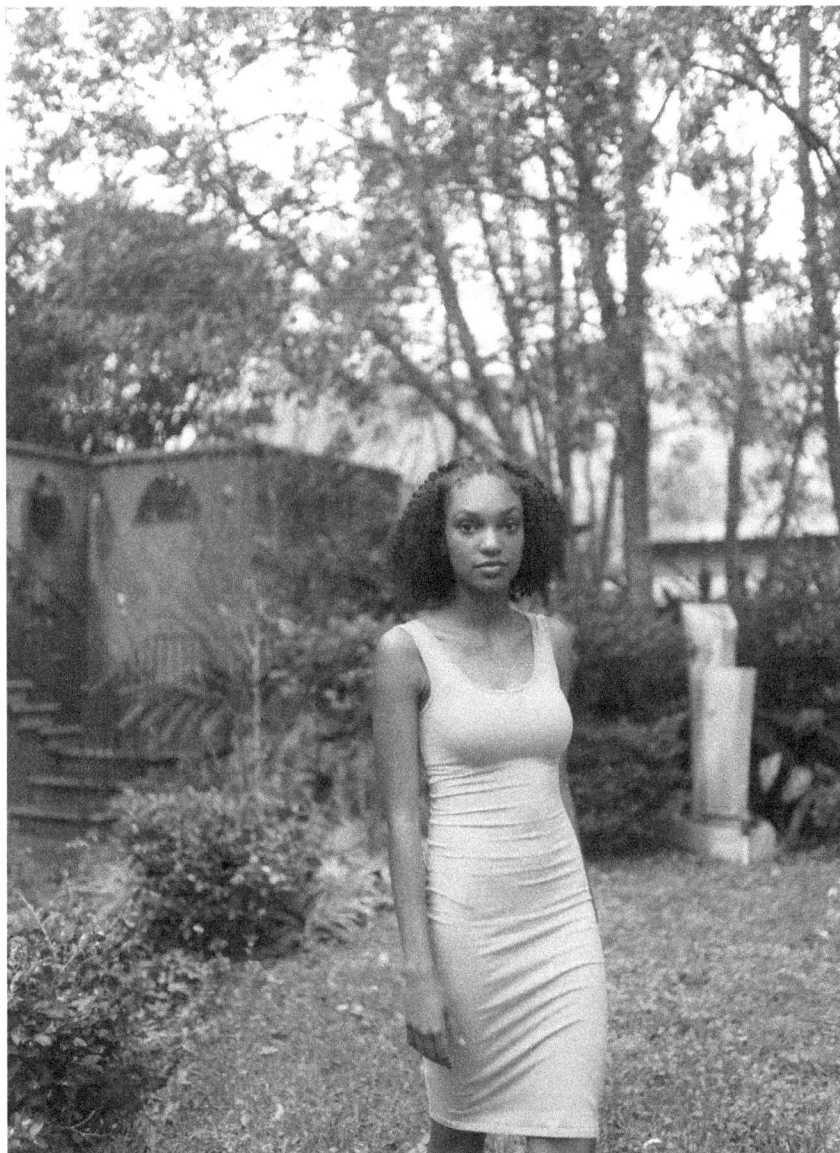

Photographed by Christian Riley. March 2022.

Photographed by Prince Pierre. July 2022

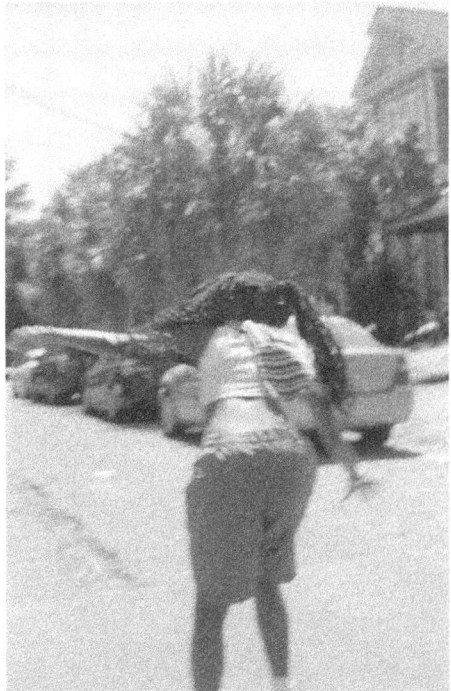

Photographed by Troy Pierre II. Sept. 2024

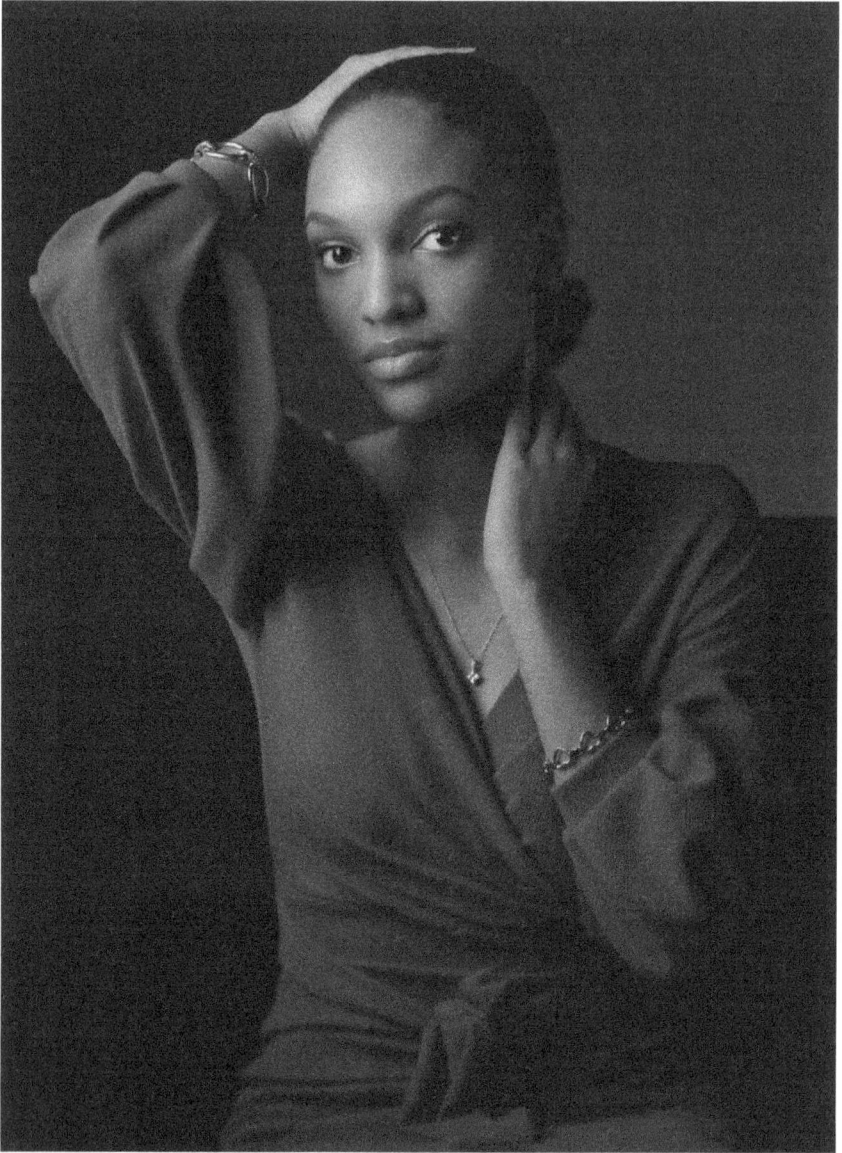

Photographed by Paul C. Jones. June 2021.

'Electric' photographed by Kerry "rexroth" Santa Cruze

Flight

I stare at the sunset
Pink and purple crowds the sky
Shapes I can't describe
Clouds so blue
I can't begin to tell you
How endless opportunities are
Beyond the thickness
The unknown
The future
Beauty swallows our narrow mind whole
Dream bigger
See the picture
Pink
Purple
Blue
Shades
Of
Boundless
Sky

We are destined to fly.

Caged

I haven't gotten on stage
And said what I had to say
In ages...

I haven't preached my preach or
Extended my reach for
Days upon days
I've felt caged

I feel the need to overflow
What's been bestowed
Pouring out of my throat
Feel the need to control
The changes

Here to uproot
The relit match to an old fruit
Quick to regroup
Im through
The stepping grounds of old roots
I sit aloof
Writing the sounds
On these pages

I'm anxious
To say this
I feel ageless

Outdated
To date
Live hate this
Spontaneous
Let's mate

Wish fate lived
Proclaim this

I stain the clean sheet
With words broader than the general

I wrote down words
But still can't tap into the subliminal

Message I sent
Not delivered. It's original

My heart is pouring
On the paper, don't think I didn't know

PinPoint

Can you do me a favor?
Can you draw?
I want you to use the sharpest pen and
Draw a thumb tack on my back and
Press hard
Push it in the wall
We won't break.
Grab the clock and hang it
It's not break.

You just nailed a clock to my back
Was I supposed to not feel that?
Am I not supposed to feel
Push harder
Lets push my limits
Help me feel the words I can't say
More pressure
Press harder
Prick me til I scream
Press harder
Acupuncture the part of me that's trying to heal
Feel whole
Fill the hole with the tack!

Can you see?
Did you do it?

Can you pin point the pens point in the part that pains
Can you pinpoint my ache?
Where it hurts?
Where the wounds still tender?

Balloon Crew

Sometimes we take breaks
And on that break we learn how to release
To let go
To rid the stored box
To remove all judgement
And watch it wash into the wonderland
To wish it well into the well that says 'swell'
To watch it fall and when it fell the fell swells
To push it far into a pale it yelled for help
To risk it all into a well the wail sounds well
In fact a wall wiped round in spell real sales well
While in the fall the rail sails out in the hell spell

Dumfound
Appalled
Stood stared
In awe
Jump back
The fall

Took care
It all
Will stared
He fought
One night
Roll raw

Hornet sting buzz bracket balloon crew
The bite rings the bell rings
The whole crew news to
You here I'm here well nobody needs you
Connie cut the string two times the balloons flew

About directing:

You have to put yourself in that headspace
If your heart isn't in it, you're not doing it right
If you don't feel it
If it's not intense
If your heart doesn't beat out of your chest
If it's not warm like a hot towel on moist skin
If it doesn't make you sweat
Make you cry
Make you nervous
Feel a rush
Make you jump
Out
Of
Your Skin
It ain't Kin

Heartbeat

There's so much shit on my heart
The bass fell flat
It weighs heavier than an elephants ass
It beats faster than tap shoes in sequence
It screams louder your aunt in a worship service
It loves harder than Martin loves Gina
It surprises me

It gets warm like I can't catch my breath
Like the rhythm is so fast I don't know if it can slow down
Like I need to cool down
Like my heart needs to stop fucking around
And get out of town
And take a pause
But don't stop

Cause that's scary
Cause I don't know what most scared me
Cause why can't my heart beat regular?
Like I'm not a regular bitch
Like let your hand touch my chest
My heart gonna snitch
And say that im that bitch
Who fell too deep too fast
Who can't get her heart out her ass
Who thinks that every time it opens up it's gonna crash
And not last
It's fallen too deep in the past
It beats to outlast the crash

So when I see a heart it's never perfect
The arc is too round
The point is too sharp
But how can one have a perfect heart?

Mine beats fast after too much coffee
After a long day
Even if no one saw me
My heart beats
And beats
And beats
And it's bass
Thumps
And knocks
And doesn't stop

And it reminds me that it's working
Even if the beat is to tell me that it's hurting
I thank God everyday that it's working

Conversation on Completion

He says I don't know how to relax
"Every moment isn't long enough
      The second lasts a minute
            And there just aren't enough hours of the day"
I say
As I shuffle back and forth of the 23rd hour on my feet
"I can do it
      I enjoy taking on projects"

"You like completion.
      How often do you start something and not finish it?"

"Very rarely"

"Just be still,
      Relax"

                  "I will,
                        Later"

Electric

I am electric
Like electricity
I plug in and out
I am power
A vibrant
Shock
Full of surprises

Cries 4 Gaza

Gaza Gaza don't you cry
In our hearts you'll never die

Biden Harris can't you see
Palestine will be free

Biden Harris you can't hide
We charge you with genocide

By the millions by the billions
We are all Palestinians

Free free Palestine

From the river to the sea
Palestine will be free

Up up with liberation
Down down with occupation

We don't want two states
We want 1948

Resistance is justified
When Palestine is occupied

From Palestine to New Orleans

Everytime the media lies
A neighborhood in Gaza dies

Israel bombs USA PAYS
HOW MANY kids did they kill today

Not another nickel not another dollar
No more money for Israel's slaughter

Reflections

Lots of reflections
Looking in the mirror
"Who is that girl?"
Do I recognize her?
"Is she who I am?"
Who I am destined to be?
"All I ever wanted?"
All I know is she's me.

Just free.

Let loose from the lies of life's lists
That get lost long later before love arrives.
Long later before love lies in the light of lust
Left lonely labeled like, not love, listen

For the dove

Outside the window
Screams chirping
They're lurking
Looking through the glass
At my reflection
Of me

Shots

Not to be mindlessly thrown back
But aimed with precision
Not to kill
Or harm
Or any drive of foul play

Clocked in the red light
Aimed
With
Precision
A decision
Must be made
So the vision
Will not fade

You miss 100% of the shots you don't take
So I pull out my stick
And pray my hand wont shake

I call this next era shots

Not to be mindlessly thrown back
Aimed with precision
Not to kill, or harm
Or be driven by foul play

I'm shooting my shot this season
It requires intense focus on the vision

Shot by a red light
Caught in the red sight
Dot down my dread spine
Got so I read fine
Mocked so I bled wine
Forgot how I said shine

I call this next era shots
Not to be mindlessly thrown back

Brown Fingers

They play the piano
     paint
     pull the trigger
     push buttons
     roll up weed
     do hair
     cook greens
     ...

Embodiment

"Society created the words
Patriarchy
Racism
Humans created that
They said this is acceptable
what's allowed
and anything that's not that is the minority
When did we become the minority?
We are not minute."

They're killing Palestinians

They'll kill your father
Your brother
Your sister
Your mother
They'll gather you all in a circle with you in the middle and
Bam shoot one in the back
Bam shoot one in the leg
Then another in the head
Until it's just you standing over the dead bodies
They'll keep you alive
Put you in the concentration camp
Even though your only 5
They want you to feel the pain
In the pit of your stomach
They want the last image of your family to scar and stain
Blood paints the ground the deepest dark red
If you can run to the corner to get to safety
They want you to know that you are next.

Thoughts at 1 am

The cars outside are loud
I wonder where they're going
Why am I still awake?
I don't remember the last earthquake
Wait...
2011, I was in 6th grade
Upper Marlboro, Maryland
My fourth grade teachers names
Alexis Pike and Carol Holding-Smith
She let us have pet crayfish, spelled with a Y
Why do I remember this?
Why am I still awake?

Where are those people going outside?
What's open at 1am on a Monday night?
Technically Tuesday morning
But a continuation of Mondays evening
Into the morning
Because both night and day can be dark
The sun shines and the moon hides
Day and night
revealing truth
Things happens in the dark
And there always comes the light
Despite the fight til
Morning
We're mourning
Bright sunlight
So keep it dark
All night
So only I can wake tomorrow's light

To be. A Concept.

To be seen
To be big
To be out of the box
To be daring
To be loud
To be dramatic

To be observed
To be small
To fit in the box
To be truth
To be quiet
To be subtle

To laugh
To smile
To cry
To scold
To be heartbroken at once while in love

To be anxious
To sweat
To burp
To pray
To move your body free of-

To be a character
A
Person
With human mistakes

To breathe freely and
Blink at a humanly pace

This is the act of love

Loose Change

Heel to toe
Step one foot over the crack
I really love my mother's back
Don't push me off of the edge
Or make me run
Hop, skip or jump
This ain't double Dutch
It's a 98 degree fuss
White fingers drip down to her clutch
And grips the locket til it grows sensitive to touch
Out pours her loose change, keys and such
And little ole me across the street— hush

Don't say a word
Don't breathe a peep
If I lift a finger
The long jacket men will leap
Stare off for seconds until the white woman blinks
And screams
And hollers and cries and shrieks

Take off
I'm sprinting with two left feet
Dogs and batons behind me
as their long jackets sweep
the concrete that was made to separate
this side from that street
But the long jackets leaped
At me and I think
I can't outrun police

Out
        of
                        breath
in this
            heat

                                    But this was my side of the street
                                            Filled with cracks
                                            And spots and stains
                                        And memories of neighbors
                                        I can't remember their names
                                    Who stood on the street like me
                                Watching white women count change
                                        Whose loosey daisy fingers
                                Rather count my life in exchange
                                    For the truth not disguised
                                    In those seconds we locked eyes

                                            Click

                                            Clack

                                            Click

                                        clack click clack
                                I'm stepping on all the cracks
                            I realized I was at the end of the line

                                            Heel to toe
                                            Heel toe
                                            Heal.
                                            Told
                                    The call to my mothers woe

                        My life cost more than all her change combined

1960Change

1962
Shirley MacLaine
Late whispers of The Children's Hour
"stay in your lane"

Those Two for the Seesaw
It's unorthodox
Unnatural

To Kill This Mockingbird
A song sung simply
"I swear I saw…"

No one ever saw
Or heard
Or listened to us

Or remembered what happened on the bus
Freedom Rides
Gathered the Cadillac Crew

Sit-in
Pro-test
Non-violent
No rest

Black Nationalism
Next year March on Washington
Stampede the stations

With color
And Women
And Colored Women

ChangeMakers

Ruby Bridges
Angela Davis
Maya Angelou
Assata Shakur
Rosa Parks
Martin Luther King Jr.
Malcom X
Langston Hughes
Amiri Baraka
Nelson Mandela
Shirley Chisholm
Harriet Tubman
Katherine Johnson
Duke Ellington
Mahalia Jackson
Lorraine Hansberry
Eartha Kitt
Nat Turner
Josephine Baker
Ella Fitzgerald

Lynn Nottage
Suzan Lori-Parks
Nikki Giovanni
August Wilson
Madam CJ Walker
Michelle Obama
Alicia Garza
Patrisse Cullors
Opal Tometi
Viola Davis
Harry Belafonte
Paul Robeson
Huey P. Newton
Fred Hampton
Gil Scott-Heron
Muhammad Ali
Sonia Sanchez
James Baldwin
Micheal Jackson

Under the Rug

Genocides   Rape cases   Black birth medical statistics

Mass shootings   Power dynamic relationships   Old family members

Kidnappers   Groomed young girls   Broken nails

Hair   Lint   Felons 4 President   Dirt   Crumbs

Old receipts   Rubber bands   Earring backs   Dead bugs

Whatever they don't want you to see
is under the rug

Hair 4C

My hair so 4C
For see the future
If you can see through my coils and kinks
So thick I could barricade
Police from facial recognition
So big I block buses
From picking up only white stock

My hair so strong
It breaks every chain
Every comb or brush used to rake
Through struggle, strands overcame
Injustice
they don't trust us
With hair this big
They can't see our every move
They can't predict our style
They can't halt our groove
Or make our work worthwhile

My hair speaks volume
Shouts to people in my silence
They wonder
Wondering why
Wondering what I did to deserve the death stare today
Wondering how my hair shimmer shine cop lights glare today
Extra circles around my block heat protectant
I mean he protecting today
I'm so fye
I'm on flames
Hair so wide
He lost aim

Big, Block, Bus
Black, Barricade
Cant see the same

Because Afro reads
Black ho needs
Natural seeds
Pack growth frees
Black folk sings

Reparations swim through my strands
Together united they stand and take hands
And love the land
I love the
Black
Hair
Band

My hair so 4C
She got 3B
And 4B
My hair 4C

My hair so 4C
It can for see
What's fo me
My hair so 4C

The second you love
Your coils and kinks
You realize 4C
Will set you free.

Anxiety

Furrowed brow
a frog in my throat
Jumping
Rattling
Choking me.

Time

In the shift of the night
Clock strikes
12:00am
The 59th second of the minute
Ran out
And boom
New Day
Oh how time works
Clock strikes
Boom
Shift of Night
New Day
Boom
Clock Strikes
Boom New Day
Boom New Day
Boom
Boom
Boom

Sirens roared down the street
During the self tape set
We all worried about the streets
On the self tape set

I actually caught the time
For once I went chasing and landed
My eyes opened and saw
The shift of the night
In plain sight
Right before my eyes
Zero chased the nine

And boom
Caught ya
Boom clock strikes
12:00am
Saw it again

12:12 turned to thirteen
My double vision
Is on a mission
Intuitions got an itchin'
To watch time pass
Takes a keen eye
'America's Best' Sale
America's BEST Sell
America's Best CELL

We're locked in the concept of time
There's not enough
We're stuck
I'm stuck in time's lapse
Around the sun for fun
While we wait in the dark?

Illusions of time
Slip through the mind
They slip through mine
And slide under the rug
Like rape charges sitting in front of a judge
Heard things get better with time
I heard it heals

I heard its heels
Sneaking down the hallways
Click Clack
I heard it kills
Time's a drug
It runs out of seconds in the field
It loses money

Loses family
So keep on running

Cause Boom
Again
Boom
A shift
Boom
She's coming
Boom
It's time
Boom
It's Tiiiiiiiiiime
Boom
For a New Day

I saw 12:34. Shift. Ended at 12:36 on 1/27/25

That's a measure of time.

Good things come to those who wait
For what? time?
The right time?
When the time is right?
In the night time?
What we waste?
But rest
It's the right time
It's the night time
While we wait.

My urge to touch pen to paper was pulsing
Popping out of my skin
Purple blue veins
And for an assessment of time?

How do you feel?
Is time on your side?

Monday at Sunset

Spider webs glisten
Birds cry
Water waves
High
...
Hello
Sun
Shining your heat on my cheek
Two birds fly over the water
With opposite direction
Where should we go?
Together?
Alone?
A low roar builds in my left ear
A boat approaches
The sun's rays draw a line through the water
I'm at the point of the other end
A five leveled boat crosses over the line
Where are we going?
Trains wail in the distance
A crane shifts on the other side
Cigarette smoke travels to my nose
My cup of tea nestled tight in my left boot
Waves lift the sticks tied to the shore
They move
Synchronized
Like breath
Marijuanna coughs echo
A squirrel hops and climbs up
Where are we going?
A tree, vibrant with green leaves stands
Feet away from a falling brown branch

Cold, decayed, weeping
The crane calls across the water
Birds fly in pairs
Conversations blur in the background
Where are we going?

Summer '08

My adult brain
Remembers

No school   Scorching hot sun
                                        "Outside"
        Sister
                            Her grandma
Peanut butter jelly sandwich
                    Stuck on the toilet- in need of mineral oil
                                                    Grandma Gloria
Kids screaming
            "Can we go outside?"
                                        Mom's at work
A burst fire hydrant
                                            Impromptu block party
                        Car doors ajar
            Radio blasting
Wishing I had a bathing suit
        Fun
                            Chasing the chimes of the ice cream truck
Sister's Grandma
                            Gloria
        Street lights turned on   Inside
A bath together
                    Sister and I
                            Dimly lit wooden house
Grandma's car- white Mitsubishi Galant

I can't tell if it was one day, one week, or one month we spent with
Grandma Gloria.

It's all a blur

Recollect   Memories   Moments

I did spend time with her?   It was Summer '08   ?

Grandma Gloria passed away in Summer 2013.
I remember my sister's tears.

www.ingramcontent.com/pod-product-compliance
Lightning Source LLC
Chambersburg PA
CBHW031002090426
42737CB00008B/638